PUBLIC TRANSPORTATION IN PARIS

Public Transportation in Paris

Third Edition

Anthony Atkielski

2022

© 2022 Anthony Atkielski. All rights reserved.

First print edition 2018. Third print edition 2022.

ISBN   979-8-35566-561-6

27 26 25 24 23   12 11 10 9 8 7 6 5 4 3

Although the author has made his best effort to ensure that information contained in this guide is timely and correct, he cannot be responsible for accidental errors and omissions.

Cover art by the author

Contents

Preface vii

Introduction 1
   Overview 2
   The Métro 3
   The RER 5
   The commuter train network 6
   The bus network 7
   The tram network 9
   Other public transportation 9

Paying for your trips 11
   The Navigo card 12
   Ticket inspections 15
   Paying for the Métro 16
   Paying for the RER and suburbs 16
   Paying for the bus 17

Finding your way 19
   Getting around in the Métro 19
   Getting around on the RER 23
   Getting around on a bus 25
   Getting to and from the airports 26
   Moving about in the suburbs 27
   An example: Getting to Disneyland Paris 29

Miscellaneous information 33
   Access for the disabled 33
   Security in the Métro 34
   Regulations, schedules, amenities 36
   Métro etiquette 39

French-English glossary 40

Notes 49

Preface

I wrote what evolved into the first edition of this little book almost forty years ago, as a guide for colleagues and friends visiting Paris. It started out as just a sheet of instructions. Over the years I continually revised and expanded it. With the development of direct print-on-demand publishing, it has finally became practical to make the book available to a wider audience.

I eventually added a glossary, because there are many signs that one sees on public transportation in Paris that are specific to that environment and are not adequately translated by standard dictionaries.

Most guides to public transportation in Paris are essentially maps with captions. I decided to write a guide without a map, but with very detailed instructions instead, much as I would have liked to have had in hand during my first visit to Paris, decades ago.

The third edition of this guide is set in larger type to facilitate consultation on the go. It further emphasizes the Navigo card to reflect the elimination of cardboard tickets that began this year. It contains other new and revised information as well.

Anthony Atkielski
Paris, France
October 2022

Introduction

Paris consistently ranks first among the world's most popular tourist destination cities, with over 50 million visitors a year.[1] One consequence of this is that many aspects of typical city life—mundane things that would be completely unremarkable in Lompoc or Sheboygan—are major tourist attractions in the French capital. Travel writers mesmerized by the City of Light wax eloquent over activities as ordinary as buying a *crêpe* or sipping coffee in a cafe. The magical spell of the city even persuades some sightseers to visit the *sewers* of Paris—and convinces them to pay for the privilege.[2]

One Parisian attraction that also happens to be eminently practical is its superlative public transportation. The city's sprawling system of rail and road mass transit is cheap and convenient, and it transports nearly ten million[3] commuters each day—more than the entire population of Switzerland.[4] It's an integral part of Parisian culture, and a fixture of daily life for the locals. It can also be a source of memories for visitors to Paris if they choose to use it. In particular, one might even say that you haven't really been to Paris until you've used the most iconic part of its public transportation, the venerable *Métro* (subway or underground).[5]

This transportation system works so well that two thirds of the city's inhabitants don't even have a car. There is no need. Everything in Paris that isn't already within easy walking distance is only a short Métro ride away. Parisians and local businesses routinely specify the nearest Métro station when giving directions; and for a local, the mention of a particular station frequently conjures up a mental picture of the neighborhood that it serves. Many Parisians immediately associate the station Cluny-La Sorbonne[6] with the heart of the Latin Quarter, and think of the huge Printemps and Galeries Lafayette department stores when someone mentions the Havre-Caumartin station adjacent to them.

Given all this, you might think that tourists would be positively eager to use mass transit during their visits to Paris—and yet many visitors avoid it.[7] They may not realize how handy it is, or they may not understand how it works, or they may even be afraid of it—especially if they come from places that are not blessed with subways, trams, and buses. This unfortunate reality was one inspiration for the book you are reading, the idea being that perhaps a clear and detailed explanation of the transit system would encourage more visitors to use it. The emphasis herein is on the city's subway system, which is the part most useful to visitors, but the other dimensions of mass transit (other rail transport, buses, and trams) are touched upon as well.

So, if you are visiting Paris (or planning a visit), and you'd like to get around town the way the Parisians do, read on.

Overview

Most of the daily commuter traffic in and around Paris is carried by trains. There are four interconnected rail networks. The one you are most likely to use is the *Métro,* an underground train system of the type you see in other large cities, such as New York or London. The Métro serves all of the city proper, with a few extensions outside the city limits. Complementing the Métro is a faster "express" subway system, called the *RER,*[8] which serves not only the city itself but also the suburbs. Beyond the RER, there is a commuter train system that serves more distant suburbs, but you won't need it within Paris itself.[9] And finally, there's the national rail network, which you would use to travel to a completely different city, domestically or abroad. We'll restrict ourselves mostly to the Métro and RER in this guide.

Since the Métro was the first subway system in France, its name has become a generic term in French for any kind of public rail transportation. So when Parisians refer to "taking the Métro," they may actually be referring to any part of the system that runs on rails (Métro, RER, or possibly a tram).

In addition to all its rail networks, Parisian mass transportation includes a very large fleet of buses. The bus network is slower than the Métro, but it's also more scenic. Bus stops are more numerous and more closely spaced in the city than Métro stations. Buses are also a good choice for people with limited mobility, since they have no steps and can accommodate wheelchairs (more on this later).

There are also nearly a dozen tramway lines[10] in Paris. These are a sort of cross between a train and a large articulated bus, running on rails at street level. They serve the perimeter of the city and don't go through the areas that tourists prefer to visit, so we won't talk much about them in this guide. In terms of pricing and use, they follow the pattern of the Métro, which we will describe in detail.

Mass transit in and around Paris is managed by a bewildering array of semi-governmental organizations. The ones you'll see mentioned most frequently are the *RATP*[11] and the *SNCF*.[12] You'll see their distinctive logos regularly when using public transportation. Their activities in Paris are organized and directed by still another organization called *IDFM*,[13] and you'll see that organization's logo now and again as well. Most of the time, you don't need to care about any of these entities.

The Métro

The Métro is what Americans call a *subway,* namely, a lightweight train that runs mostly in tunnels underground. It's similar to many other subways in the world. In fact, some of the younger subway systems around the globe were modeled on the Paris system, and sometimes they are even called *metros*.[14] The Paris Métro isn't quite the world's oldest or largest subway, but some might argue that it's the best, with sixteen lines[15] and over three hundred stations, with more planned for the future. This part of the Parisian mass-transit system is by far the most useful for tourists and visitors.

Almost all Métro stations are within the Paris city limit.[16] Each Métro line is numbered and has two parallel tracks on which trains move in opposite directions[17] at regular, frequent intervals.

The direction of a train is identified by the name of the last station on the line in that direction. You can generally make a connection between one line and another (called a *correspondance* in French) at any station served by both lines, without leaving the Métro. Each train stops at each station in its path,[18] whether there are passengers waiting or not.

You can find a Métro station within easy walking distance of any point within Paris,[19] and this network is really all you need to get quickly from place to place within the city itself.

All Métro trips cost the same amount of money. You use a special "smart card"—digitally loaded with a transit pass or individual tickets—to enter the system. You can make as many connections as you need to get from your departure point to your destination, as long as you don't actually leave the Métro, and as long as your trip is completed within 90 minutes.[20] Most trips require only a single connection, and many require none at all; trips requiring two connections are rare.[21] Because tourists usually just move about within the city rather than commute to and from the suburbs, their trips tend to be fast—perhaps ten or fifteen minutes to get practically anywhere in town.[22]

The oldest line of the Métro, Line 1, entered service more than a hundred years ago, and has undergone regular renovation and modernization. The newest line, Line 14, opened in 1999, and was the first completely automated line (*i.e.,* operated solely by computers, without drivers). Other lines, including Line 1, have gradually been automated also. A new line, Line 16, is under construction now. All of the network has been continually upgraded and expanded throughout its history.

On signs, the line numbers of the Métro are shown against a circular, color-coded background.

The Métro operates roughly from 5 AM to 1 AM, with the exact times varying from one line or station to another. The system runs every day of the year, including Saturdays, Sundays, and all holidays. Twenty-four-hour operation is under discussion but still has not been implemented at the time of this writing. On some special occasions, such as New Year's Eve, the trains may exceptionally run all night. Nevertheless, in order to be sure you don't get stranded, it's best to plan to start your last Métro ride of the day before midnight.

The RER

The RER is a network of high-speed trains that travel through Paris and continue out into the suburbs. Within the city, RER stations are much fewer in number than Métro stations, but for long commutes, the high speed of the RER compensates for the inconvenience of its fewer stations.

There are five RER lines, identified by the letters A through E. They serve 257 stations, of which all but 33 are outside Paris itself. Within Paris, lines A and E run east-west, lines B and D run north-south, and Line C does a bit of both. In contrast with most Métro lines,[23] RER lines often split into different branches after they spread out into the suburbs. RER trains are larger than Métro trains and are compatible with the national rail network. They run underground within Paris, but run above ground in the suburbs. Some RER trains, used especially during rush hours, have two levels. In other respects, the RER lines resemble those of the Métro.

On signs, the letters of the RER lines are shown color-coded and surrounded by circles.

RER stations within Paris allow for connections with any adjacent Métro lines.[24] Tickets and passes used on the Métro are also valid on the RER, within certain limits. Ticketing on the RER is based on either the starting and ending points of a trip, for individual tickets,[25] or a system of five concentric fare zones, centered on Paris, for multiple-use transit passes. The city itself is Zone 1, and any ticket providing for travel through Zone 1 also allows travel on the Métro. If you stay within Zone 1 (that is, within the city) the same ticket allows you to use the Métro and RER interchangeably, *i.e.*, you can even mix and match the two networks on a single trip. (The current trend is towards fare structures that cover all zones, all the time, and it's possible that zones will be eliminated at some point in the future.)

Administration and operation of the RER are shared between the RATP and the SNCF, with the RATP managing Line A and part of Line B, and the SNCF managing the rest of Line B, and lines C, D, and E. You may notice subtle differences between how the SNCF (which also operates the national railway network) and the RATP operate their networks. The SNCF's trains might remind you a bit of traditional cross-country railways, while the RATP has a distinctly urban, big-city feel that is more specifically Parisian.

The RER is much younger than the Métro: the first RER line passing through the city (Line A) was completed in 1977. Line E was opened in 1999. As with the Métro, upgrading and expansion of the RER is an ongoing process.

Unlike the Métro, the RER serves the airports (indirectly),[26] as well as suburban attractions such as Versailles and Disneyland.

The commuter train network

A network of commuter trains, called the *Transilien,* and operated by the SNCF, serves the Paris suburbs. It interconnects with the Métro and RER at major railway stations within Paris. It uses the same tracks as the national railway system. Trains in this network resemble conventional cross-country trains, except for obvious adaptations to the high volume and short duration of commuter traffic—there are no sleeping or restaurant cars, for example, and usually there are no toilets. The ticketing scheme for commuter trains is simpler than that used for cross-country trains, and it is designed to resemble and fit in with that of the Métro, RER, and other public-transportation systems in the Paris region.

The commuter lines serving Paris are designated by letters, similar to those of the RER. On signs, the letters are shown color-coded and surrounded by boxes, and they are assigned beginning with the letter H.[27]

The commuter trains serve certain stations at certain times, like cross-country trains. Naturally, the average trip on this network takes considerably longer than a trip on the Métro or RER, in part because of the greater distances covered, and in part because commuter trains often make a great many stops in the suburbs, and thus never build up much speed.

Commuter trains enter Paris only to stop at major railway stations, and make no other stops within the city. Métro and (usually) RER stations lurk beneath each of these conventional train stations,[28] facilitating connections between the networks.

Yes, it's a bit complicated. Fortunately, to travel within Paris or visit nearby suburban destinations, you don't need the commuter train network. In consequence, we won't be discussing it very much in this guide.[29]

The bus network

Buses are an extremely common sight in Paris, and many major streets have special bus lanes set aside for them. The RATP operates nearly three hundred bus routes, serving more than thirteen thousand bus stops in the Paris metropolitan area—amazing numbers when you consider that the city itself is only a few miles across.[30] Bus stops are much more closely spaced than Métro or RER stations, but bus routes are so circuitous and seemingly random (at least from the standpoint of a visitor) that you must know exactly where you are in the city, exactly where you are going, and exactly which bus routes lead to your destination in order to make efficient use of them. This works very well for Parisians who commute regularly over the same routes each day, but it can be tedious for the occasional visitor or tourist.

Bus routes have numbers,[31] just as subway lines and commuter trains do. In theory, they serve specific stops at specific times, but traffic in Paris is so heavy and variable that the published schedules cannot be relied upon; it's easier to just stand at a bus stop and wait for one to come along. There's often an electronic display showing when the next bus will pass, which is often every ten or twenty minutes during weekdays. Bus travel can be slow compared to the subway, since heavy traffic limits the average rush-hour speed of a city bus to about six miles per hour. Dedicated bus lanes within the city help buses to remain on time, but for pure speed, the bus still remains far behind the Métro.

On signs, bus line numbers appear on a square, color-coded background.

The main advantage of a bus for visitors is that it is considerably more scenic than the Métro, given that buses trundle about on city streets, whereas subway trains spend almost all their time zooming through tunnels. However, contrary to what some popular travel guides claim, city buses are *not* a low-cost substitute for a tour bus: they are far too crowded for sightseeing, the seats are not arranged for it, and they follow routes designed to serve areas where people live and work—not routes intended to showcase Parisian tourist attractions.

Visitors with mobility issues may prefer the bus over the Métro because buses have no steps to climb. In contrast, stairways are ubiquitous in the Métro, and are practically impossible to avoid.

A single standard ticket is good for one trip between two points on one or more buses or trams within the city. If you use a standard ticket for a bus or tram, it's not valid for connections with trains, and *vice versa*. Things gets more complicated for rides within or towards the suburbs, which occasionally require several tickets or specific point-to-point tickets. If you buy your ticket directly from the bus driver as you board, the ticket is only good for one ride on that bus—you can't make any connections. The time between your first use of a ticket on a bus and the last use of the same ticket must not exceed 90 minutes.

All of the buses within Paris are managed by the RATP. Bus routes in the suburbs are often operated cooperatively by the RATP and local suburban transportation authorities.

Unlike the Métro and RER, bus service doesn't stop completely during the night. The *Noctilien* bus service continues with 47 routes operating all night long in Paris and a few suburbs, during the period when the normal daytime buses aren't operating (from roughly 11 PM or so to 6 AM). Single-use tickets are not valid for connections between Noctilien buses, and multiple tickets are required for trips spanning more than two zones.

Line 40 of the bus network—formerly known as the *Monmartrobus*—serves the area around Montmartre and Pigalle, and is popular with tourists. It operates a fleet of smaller buses that are particularly suited to the tiny streets of the neighborhood. The line serves even the very top of the Montmartre butte, including the artists' square at the summit that is a favorite with visitors.

In other respects, it's a bus line like any other. Like all RATP bus lines, Line 40 is wheelchair-friendly, despite the slightly smaller buses.

Two special bus lines outside the main network, *OrlyBus* and *RoissyBus,* provide shuttle service to and from the airports. See *Getting to and from the airports* on page 26 for more details.

The tram network

There are twelve tramway lines in and around the city that are part of public transportation. They are designated T1 through T13.[32] They operate in essentially the same way as the Métro, with the same fare structure, but they mostly run around the perimeter of the city (when they pass trough the city at all), outside areas that are likely to be interesting to tourists. Because of this, we won't dwell on the tramway lines here. Single-use tickets, once used on the tram, are valid for connections with other trams and buses, but not trains, and vice versa.

Other public transportation

Another form of transportation included in the RATP system that is very useful to tourists is the Montmartre Funicular,[33] an inclined, outdoor elevator that takes you up the hill to the Sacré-Cœur basilica. Its turnstiles accept regular RATP tickets and passes, and it is very handy for those who don't fancy hiking up hundreds of steps in order to reach the popular Montmartre neighborhood of Paris. The Funicular runs along the west side of the park[34] in front of Sacré-Cœur, next to the many steps of pedestrian Foyatier Street. The trip up or down takes about 90 seconds.

Batobus is a small fleet of boats operated by Bateaux Parisiens (a popular operator of excursion boats in Paris) under contract to the Paris Port Authority. These boats shuttle up and down the Seine River, serving nine stops on the Right and Left Banks. They are not very practical from a pure transportation standpoint, but they are very popular with tourists, transporting a million passengers a year. Their fare system is completely independent of other transportation, and is based on (fairly expensive) "hop on, hop off" day passes.[35]

A wholly-owned subsidiary of the RATP operates a fleet of double-decker tour buses called *Tootbus* (formerly *OpenTour*), in competition with a number of other operators. The buses are completely dedicated to sightseeing; their only connection to public transportation is the fact that they are owned by the RATP. They don't accept Métro tickets or passes, and instead have a pricing scheme similar to that of Batobus.[36]

Orlyval (not to be confused with OrlyBus) is a short light-rail line that connects the RER to Orly Airport. It is described further under *Getting to and from the airports,* on page 26.

You may still encounter occasional references to *RoissyRail* and *OrlyRail* in outdated travel books. They were rail services between Paris and the airports. They were merged into Lines B and C (respectively) of the RER, some years ago.

Paying for your trips

Before you can use mass transit in Paris, you have to know how to pay for it. The transit authorities offer a vast array of fare schemes, but only a handful are practical for visitors. The entire system is heavily subsidized in order to keep it affordable for everyone, so whichever scheme you choose, mass transit in Paris is cheap. You can easily spend more on lunch for one day in Paris than you'll spend on public transportation for the whole trip.

In fact, if you're a typical tourist, coming to Paris on a once-in-a-lifetime trip from a faraway land like the USA, Australia, or India, the cost of public transportation isn't going to make much of a dent in your budget, so there's no point in fretting over it. For this reason, we base our recommendations in this guide on what will be *fast* and *convenient* for you, rather than try to recommend the rock-bottom cheapest fares. Time spent fumbling for just the right ticket at the turnstile, or trying to buy the cheapest transit pass at a busy ticket window, is time not spent exploring Paris. Besides, the differences among fares only amount to a few euro, in most cases.

With this reality in mind, then, you basically have two broadly practical options when paying for your trips: you can buy individual tickets, or you can buy a pass. Individual tickets are good for one trip each; passes can be used for multiple trips within certain time or distance limits. If you're only going to be in the city for a day or so, or if you want tickets that can be used by anyone in your group, then individual tickets are probably best. If you're staying for several days, a pass might be more convenient.

Ordinary individual tickets,[37] valid for any trip within the city limits[38] cost €2.10 each, or €16.90 for a group of ten. Tickets for trips beginning or ending *outside* the city limits vary in price depending on the arrival and departure points. If you're taking a bus, a single ticket can be bought directly from the driver, but it will cost €2.50, and it is valid only on that bus and not beyond. As for passes, they vary in price with the type of pass and its time and distance limits.

For decades, public-transit tickets consisted of little strips of cardboard with a magnetic stripe on the back. A handful of tickets are still sold in this form today, including individual tickets—if you want to buy just one—as well a few types of passes. But for the most part, these bits of stiff paper have been replaced by newer technology, in the form of "smart cards" onto which ticket and passes can be electronically loaded. These cards are sold under the brand name *Navigo*.

The Navigo card

Navigo cards exist in several flavors. The simplest is the aptly-named *Navigo Easy*. It costs €2 (a one-time fee), and can be loaded with individual tickets (including tickets for the RoissyBus and OrlyBus airport shuttles) or a daily pass. It can be reloaded as required, and the card itself is reusable for ten years. It can be shared among the members of your group, but *not at the same time for the same trip*—so if several of you are traveling together on the Métro, each of you will need to have his own Navigo on his person while inside the system.

You can buy a Navigo card at any station on the system that has a ticket window staffed by a human being. You can then load it up with tickets or a pass, at the ticket window or at a ticket machine. The machines speak English, whereas ticket vendors often do not.

Inside Paris, individual trip fares are the same no matter where you are going or how you are getting there. Outside Paris, fares can vary for each trip, depending on the departure and arrival stations of the trip, and sometimes on the type of transportation. This means that, if you opt for individual tickets, a given ticket will work for any trip within Paris; but if you venture outside Paris, you'll need a specific ticket for your destination for each trip.[39] Incidentally, there are no round-trip tickets *per se;* instead, you just use two tickets, one for travel each way.

In contrast with individual tickets, passes allow for unlimited travel within a specific geographical area and during a specific time period. The most popular ones can be loaded onto a Navigo. There are some that exist only as cardboard tickets.

Some passes are loaded onto a slightly different cad, the Navigo Découverte. It costs €5, and is also valid for a decade. It can be loaded with a weekly, daily, or monthly pass. The Navigo Découverte comes with an ID card that requires a small photo—which you can buy from a photo booth in most stations, if you don't already have one (this increases the one-time cost of the card by several euro). The Navigo Découverte can be used only by the person identified on the ID card. Ticket inspectors may ask to see both the Navigo and the ID card, so keep them together.

The Navigo card has other flavors, too, but they are either sold only to residents (ensured by a requirement for a permanent local address or bank reference) or they are simply impractical for someone who is just visiting.

The simplest passes, called *forfaits,* are available for a day, a week, or a month.[40] The daily variety can be loaded onto a Navigo Easy or Découverte, but the other two can be loaded only onto a Navigo Découverte. A weekly pass always covers Monday to Sunday, and a monthly pass always covers one calendar month, no matter when these passes are purchased or first used.

The fares for passes often depend on their geographic coverage. For this purpose, the Paris metropolitan area is divided into five concentric fare zones, centered on Paris. Zones 1 and 2 cover all of Paris and the outer reaches of the Métro. Zones 1 through 5 cover everything except some airport transportation (Orlyval and the shuttles—see *Getting to and from the airports,* on page 26).

Sifting through all of this, we can narrow the options down to two potentially suitable choices for the average traveler: either a Navigo Easy loaded with, say, ten tickets to start, for €16.90 (plus the €2 cost of the card, if you don't already have one); or a Navigo Découverte loaded with a weekly pass for all zones, for €30.00 (plus the €5 cost of the card, and several euro for a photo, if you don't already have these). The first option lets you make ten trips anywhere in Paris but not the suburbs, without an expiration date; the second option lets you make unlimited trips for one week or month in both Paris and the suburbs, including Versailles, the airports (except as previously noted), and Disneyland.

There is also a pass that we *cannot* recommend, and that is the notorious *Paris Visite,* an overpriced pass that is aimed squarely at tourists and promoted heavily by the RATP. It allows unlimited travel for one to five consecutive days on any form of transport, within a specific range of zones. This sounds good—except that it's really expensive. Prices start at €13.55 for one day only and inside Paris only, and rise rapidly from there.[41] There are very few situations in which you can gain anything by buying this pass. We mention it only because ticket agents may try to pressure you into buying it.

There are many other passes, catering to seniors, young people, students, the unemployed, and others, but they are either ill-suited to the needs of visitors or simply unavailable to them entirely, so we'll skip them.

As we have indicated, if you do not already have the physical Navigo card itself, you must add the cost of buying one to the cost of your first Navigo pass. For the Navigo Découverte, the cost is €5, and you'll also need to buy a passport-style photo to stick onto the Navigo card (unless you already have one handy). There are photo booths in many stations that can help you to obtain this, for several euro. The Navigo Easy does not require a photo, and costs only €2. Ticket agents can also usually provide a rigid clear-plastic holder for either card if you ask for one, which can be handy if you don't plan to keep the card protected in a wallet. Unlike cardboard tickets, Navigo cards are not harmed by magnetic clasps on purses or bags.

After a pass expires or you run out of tickets, you can just load a new pass or tickets onto the card. Ticket machines and ticket windows have a device that does this when you make your purchase.

To use a Navigo card, just hold it over the purple target on the turnstile. The card is readable even in a holder or wallet: Parisians often keep it in their bags or purses and simply wave these past the purple targets to pass through the turnstiles (this takes a bit of practice). A turnstile beeps when it has successfully read the card, and if it's a Navigo Easy, the turnstile will display the number of tickets remaining on the card. Since the Navigo card itself is valid for ten years, you can take it home and reuse it if you return to Paris within a decade.

Ticket inspections

Within the rail networks, there is what the transit authorities call the *zone contrôlée,* meaning the "controlled area." It's the part of the system within which you're expected to be in possession of a ticket or pass that is valid for your trip. You use your ticket or pass to enter the controlled area through the turnstiles, and at the end of your trip, you exit the controlled area through automatic doors or turnstiles.[42]

You must keep your ticket or pass handy within the controlled area, in case ticket inspectors ask to see it; if you can't produce it when asked, you risk having to pay a €50 fine[43] to the inspector on the spot. Being a tourist will not get you off the hook—the transit agents have seen too many tourists who deliberately defraud the system and then plead ignorance. Expect no leniency, and follow the rules.

When you enter this area through a turnstile, the system records the time and station at which you entered. Ticket inspectors will check this time to make sure you haven't been loitering about for hours and haven't tried to reuse a single-use ticket. Don't enter the system without validating your ticket or pass with a turnstile.

Ticket inspectors are uniformed (a distinctive business suit) and work in groups. Plainclothes transit police are also normally posted discreetly nearby, to deal with the small minority of fraudsters who become aggressive.

Your ticket or pass can be checked on buses, too, so make sure you have it validated and on hand there as well.

Be forewarned that personal items such as handbags or wallets that incorporate magnetic clasps can demagnetize and ruin cardboard tickets, so keep the latter away from the former. Navigo cards are safe.[44]

Paying for the Métro

In all Métro stations, there is at least one ticket machine, and the machines can function in English. Actual windows with human agents selling tickets are increasingly hard to find. You can buy individual cardboard tickets and reload Navigo cards with tickets or passes at both machines and ticket windows, but the smart cards themselves must be initially purchased at a window (you can reload them at a machine thereafter). Ticket windows accept cash and plastic. So do machines, except that some machines accept coins but not banknotes. You may need your PIN to use a credit card, and be forewarned that some non-French credit cards without built-in chips may not work.

In an increasing number of stations, the RATP agents behind the window, if any, are there only to answer questions and provide what the RATP mysteriously calls "after-sales service." In these stations, you'll have to buy your ticket from a machine. If the word *Vente* or *Billets* appears over the window, the human being inside still sells tickets—otherwise he is just there to provide information.

Paying for the RER and suburbs

The payment procedures for the RER and commuter trains are about the same as those for the Métro, and the tickets are largely interchangeable for trips within Paris, particularly between the RER and the Métro. You can either buy a ticket specifically for the trip you wish to take (from a ticket window or a machine), or you can buy one of the previously mentioned passes with the appropriate zones on it.

The monthly pass is "dezoned" on weekends, holidays and school vacations, and from mid-July to mid-August, which means that it works in all zones, 1 to 5, during these periods, no matter which zones it was purchased for.

In contrast to the Métro, in the RER you have to pass through turnstiles that require your ticket or pass when entering *and* when exiting the system. If you don't have a valid ticket or pass at the exit, you're stuck. If you're exiting the system completely with a single-use ticket, the turnstile may keep it—this is normal, not a malfunction.[45]

Paying for the bus

Payment methods for the bus within Paris are the same as those for the RER and Métro, since the same tickets and passes are used.

Tickets must be inserted into a small machine near the entrance of the bus. The machine will illuminate a green light and beep if it is pleased with the ticket. If you have a Navigo card, you can simply wave it at the purple target near the entrance door as you board the bus, and it will also beep cheerfully with a green light. Most buses can only be boarded from the front door; the other doors are used as exits only, except on articulated buses. Strollers and wheelchairs must board from the other door, as they won't fit past the front door, but their owners are still expected to validate their passes or tickets.

Standard singe-use tickets allow you to switch buses if you need to make a connection, and also allow connections with trams, but once such a ticket is used for a bus or tram, it can't be used for connections with trains; and *vice versa*.[46] That is, you can use such a ticket to make bus or tram connections if you start your trip on a bus or tram, or you can use it to make train connections if you start your trip on rail transport—but you can't use the *same* ticket to connect between buses/trams and rail transit. Passes do not have these confusing restrictions, which is another good reason to buy a pass.

If you buy an individual ticket directly from the bus driver, that ticket is good only on that bus, for that trip—you'll need a new ticket if you wish to use any other part of the transit system. Tickets bought from the driver are also more expensive than tickets bought elsewhere: a single ticket from the bus driver will cost you €2.50, even though it doesn't allow any connections.

Finding your way

Once you know how to pay for your trip, the next step is to learn how to find your way from one place to another using the various networks of the system. The Métro is the easiest of the four networks to use, and it also tends to be the most useful network for visitors.

Getting around in the Métro

The first step in using the Métro is to find a Métro station entrance. Most Métro stations are underground; a few lines in a few places are elevated. Stations are clearly marked, but discreet; you may not notice them unless you are specifically looking for them. Typically they appear as nondescript stairways descending into the ground, and are identified by signs showing M or RER or MÉTRO. You can simply walk down the stairs into the station of your choice.

We've already covered the matter of paying for your trip. We'll assume that you already have the necessary Navigo card or cardboard ticket. With that in hand, look around for a map before passing through the turnstile. All stations have a large map on a wall somewhere, although it is not always obvious. You can also buy a small, plastic-coated Métro map in many bookstores or at a newsstand, and agents at Métro information windows will usually give you a very tiny map for free. Some stations have fancy lighted maps, on which you can push a button corresponding to your destination in order to see the route you must follow in order to reach it. A few stations have computerized kiosks that serve the same purpose. There are also smartphone apps that provide maps, such as the RATP's own *Bonjour* app. In any case, you need to find the station you've just entered, then find the station closest to your destination, then note the Métro line or lines connecting the two stations on the map (smartphone apps can partially automate this).[47]

After you've found the lines connecting your departure and arrival stations, you must then choose the best path between the two stations. The method varies, depending on whether the two stations are on the same or different lines.

If both stations happen to be on the same Métro line, the path is obvious: you simply take a train on that line in the direction of your destination station, and get off when you reach that station. Keep in mind that signs showing the way to a train platform identify the direction of a train by the name of the last station on the line in the direction the train is traveling. For example, on Line 1 of the Métro, the platform at which westbound trains stop will be marked DIRECTION LA DÉFENSE, because La Défense is the last station at the western end of this line. Eastbound trains on Line 1 will stop at platforms marked direction CHÂTEAU DE VINCENNES, because Château de Vincennes is the name of the station at the eastern terminus of the line.

With only two exceptions,[48] all Métro directions are unique; that is, only one Métro train in Paris travels in any given direction. Because of this, as long as you find the direction you want, irrespective of the line(s) you take, you need not worry about going the wrong way.

If your destination is not on the same line as your point of departure, you'll have to change trains somewhere during your trip. This is called a *correspondance* (connection) in French. Find the line that serves your destination, find the line that serves your point of departure, and then find a station at which the lines meet; at that station, you'll need to change trains in the direction of your destination. If the two lines do not meet at any station, you'll have to change trains twice, using a third line that serves a station on your line and a station on the destination line—but this is very unusual,[49] and in most cases only one connection is required.

Once you know how to get to the station closest to your destination, you can enter the controlled area of the Métro. Most turnstiles accept both the traditional cardboard tickets and Navigo cards. The ones that accept cardboard tickets have an obvious slot in front to accept the ticket (you can insert the ticket in any direction); the ones that accept Navigo cards have a purple target on them over which you wave the card. There will be at least one of each type at every entrance. If you are using a cardboard ticket, the machine will return your ticket from a slot on top of the turnstile. It will simply beep and show a green arrow for a Navigo, and you may then proceed. Take your ticket back if that's what you have, and walk through the turnstile. You must keep your ticket until you leave the controlled area of the Métro, in order to prove that you have paid. Spot checks by groups of uniformed RATP agents are frequent, and you'll be fined if you don't have a valid ticket. Pleading ignorance of the regulations will not allow you to escape the fine.

An unpleasant beep and a red light on the turnstile means that your ticket is not valid; usually this means that you're using a single-use cardboard ticket that you've already used on a previous trip. Other possible causes are an attempt to go outside the zone(s) allowed by the ticket or pass, or a ticket/pass that has expired, or an attempt to use a pass a second time in the same station over a short period (around ten minutes—it's a fraud-prevention measure). Cardboard tickets can also be demagnetized by the magnetic clasps of some accessories such as pocketbooks and purses, so be careful where you store your tickets.

Once inside the controlled area, the secret to success is to *read all the signs*. As long as you follow the signs, you cannot become lost. No real knowledge of French is necessary. Just look for signs mentioning the direction, station, line, or connection that you wish to take, and follow them. Maps are present on every train platform and on every train as well, in case you forget your planned itinerary.

Once you're on the platform, you need only wait for a train to arrive. This occurs as often as every 60 seconds during rush hour, and as infrequently as every ten or fifteen minutes during the slowest traffic periods (late at night on a Sunday, for example). Trains on the Métro almost always arrive from your left as you stand on the platform; be sure to stand well clear of the edge.

Some trains have doors that open only if you press a button or lift a lever on the door. The newest trains have automatic doors that open by themselves. After a brief stop in the station, a warning buzzer will sound, and the doors will close again automatically. Don't try to board the train after the buzzer sounds, as this slows traffic, especially during rush hour.

An increasing number of lines have doors on both the platform and the train, which open and close automatically and simultaneously. In some cases, the platform door opens by itself, but you may still have to press a button or lift a lever on the train door in order to open it. The system is gradually being upgraded, and eventually doors on every train will work automatically.

As you ride the train, look carefully at the station names at each stop. The name of the station is always clearly marked on large signs visible from the train. On some lines, a recorded announcement is made at each station as well. The trains also have maps of their routes on a sign over the inside doors of each car, and on newer trains lights and/or screens indicate the name of the station at which the train is currently stopped.

When the train stops at your destination station or connection station, get off. Be sure to push the button or lift the lever on the door to open it, if you are not on one of the newer trains with automatic doors. Watch how others do it if you can't figure out how to operate the door. Passengers normally exit the train on the right, with respect to the motion of the train (there are a few exceptions at the ends of some lines[50]).

If you need to make a connection, follow the signs to find your way to the next train. Signs marked CORRESPONDANCE (typically in black text on an orange background) show the way to connecting trains. Signs marked SORTIE (typically in white text on a blue background) show the way out of the Métro. Take care not to exit the controlled area of the Métro when making a connection, or you'll have to use a fresh ticket to get back in. Signs marked LIMITE DE VALIDITÉ DES BILLETS and automatic turnstiles or doors mark the exits from the controlled area.

Signs in red, marked PASSAGE INTERDIT, mean "do not enter," and if you follow them, you risk ending up on another platform, in another station, or on another planet. Signs marked SORTIE DE

SECOURS, in green, are emergency exits only; use the normal exits instead (white text on a blue background), unless there is truly an emergency.

When you arrive at your destination station, follow the SORTIE signs all the way out of the Métro. If you were traveling on a single-use ticket, you can discard it once you've left the system; if you have a pass, then obviously you'll want to keep it with you.

Getting around on the RER

The RER is just a slightly more complicated variation of the Métro. The RER is very useful if you wish to travel outside Paris, or if you need to cover a large distance within the city fairly quickly.

Direct entrances into the RER are relatively rare, since the number of RER stations inside Paris is very small compared to the number of Métro stations—so don't walk around searching for one. Instead, make a connection from the Métro to the RER at a station served by both systems. You can make connections between the Métro and the RER freely as long as you stay within the city limits.

Typically, you will make a connection between the Métro and the RER in order to move more quickly across the city. A connection in the opposite direction, from RER to Métro, will then take you to your final destination, if the RER station itself is not your destination. In practice, however, you'll find that few trips within the city itself justify connections with the high-speed RER.

The most important difference between the Métro and the RER is in the pricing of tickets. A single Métro ticket is good for any trip within the city limits, with or without RER connections. However, once you move outside the city, you'll need a ticket that matches the distance you are traveling if you plan to use the RER. This means either a single ticket that specifically names your destination station, or a pass that covers the necessary zones, based on the concentric zone system mentioned earlier in this guide. For such trips, always make sure you have the right ticket or pass for your trip, or you may end up stuck in a deserted RER station in the suburbs, with no choice but to retrace your steps and buy a new ticket.

At most stations, you must use your ticket or pass to enter *and* exit the RER. If you are not leaving the system, the turnstile will return your ticket to you. If you are leaving the RER and the system, the turnstile will usually keep your ticket, if it's a single-use ticket. If you are leaving the RER but continuing on the Métro, the turnstile will return your ticket. A turnstile that beeps unpleasantly is usually a turnstile that isn't happy with your ticket—often because you have traveled beyond the zone limits of the ticket, or because you've mixed up your tickets and you are trying to get out with a ticket different from the one you used to get in. You can't get out of the RER without a valid ticket, so be careful.

Unlike Métro trains, on which you usually enter and exit cars on the right side of the train with respect to the direction of travel, RER trains may load or unload passengers from either side, depending on the station—so be sure to observe carefully as you arrive at your destination station to determine which side is the side from which you'll get off. They don't always arrive from the left as seen from the platform, either, so be alert. During low-traffic periods, short trains may be in service (look for TRAIN COURT on the lighted departure displays—*court* means "short"). When this is the case, be sure that you're standing close to the center of the platform, or you may find that the train stops fifty feet away from you, and you'll have to sprint to get aboard, or wait for another train.

Métro trains stop at every station on their respective lines, but this is not true for RER trains. All RER trains stop at every RER station on their lines within Paris, but stations outside of Paris may only be served by every third or fourth train. Lighted destination boards on the platform indicate the stations served by each arriving train; the wise traveler consults these boards before boarding a train for the suburbs, so as to avoid surprise excursions to Versailles or Bangkok.

Most RER lines split into several branch lines as the main line reaches the suburbs. Once again, you must be careful to take a train that continues on to the branch you want, if you are going outside the city. The destination stations indicated on the platform will usually make it obvious which branch of the line is being served by an arriving train; announcements in the train are usually also made before the branch is taken, if you understand spoken French. The newer RER trains have lighted displays inside, over the doors, that show the current station and the other stations that will be served by the train.

Getting around on a bus

The bus system in Paris works extremely well for the city's residents, but it can be frustrating for the visitor, because it requires an intimate knowledge of the layout of the city and of the bus routes in question. However, it is more scenic than the subway, if time is not a concern, and provided that you know exactly where you are and where you are going. Additionally, if you have problems climbing or descending stairs (unavoidable in the Métro), the bus system may be more practical; all city buses are designed without steps and can accept wheelchairs.

Bus stops are plentiful in Paris. Most bus stops are mandatory, meaning that the bus will always stop there if there is someone waiting. Other stops are optional, meaning that the bus will stop only if you gesture to the bus indicating that you want to board. The mandatory stops usually include a covered bus stop (the *Abribus);* optional stops may simply have a sign on a pole.

Check the maps at each bus stop to see the stops served by the bus you want to take. Verify that an approaching bus has the route number that you need for your destination. Board the bus at the front. Wave your Navigo card at the purple target on the machine just inside the doors; it will beep with a green light of approval. If you're using a cardboard ticket, insert it into the machine behind the driver, and it will beep and return the ticket.

A display near the ceiling at the front of the bus will announce each stop as you approach it. There may be a voice announcement as well. When you see your stop approaching, look for a red button on one of the stainless-steel railings or columns in the bus, and press it; this signals the driver that someone wishes to get off at the next stop—otherwise he may not stop unless people are waiting to get on. When the bus stops, you can get off. Exit via the rear door(s), not via the front door.

If you need to change buses or connect with a tram, you can use the same ticket, as long as it has been less than 90 minutes since you first used the ticket—and provided that it is not a ticket that you bought from the bus driver (those are only good on the bus where they are purchased).

You can stand or sit on the bus (and on the Métro). Some seats are reserved on public transportation for war veterans, handicapped persons, etc., so occasionally someone might ask you to move if you are in one of these seats.

Practically all public buses today are wheelchair-friendly. They can generally tilt or extend a ramp for wheelchairs if you get the driver's attention. Wheelchairs and strollers can board from the rear doors (as there is no room to do so in front), but you still have to validate your ticket or pass.

Some large, articulated buses have multiple entrances and exits, with multiple ticket/Navigo machines.

A handful of bus routes (*e.g.,* those serving the airports) require either special tickets with separate pricing or multiple/special tickets priced according to the distance you wish to cover.

Getting to and from the airports

If you are visiting Paris from the United States, chances are that you will enter and leave France by air. If you have any luggage, a taxi or airport shuttle is by far the most practical way to get to and from the two passenger airports serving Paris (Charles de Gaulle airport to the north of the city, and Orly airport to the south).

If you have little or no luggage, however, be advised that the mass-transit systems of Paris do serve the airports—indirectly. RER Line C serves Orly (that is, there is a shuttle from the Aéroport d'Orly station to the airport itself). A fully automated, somewhat expensive, rubber-tired Métro-like line, called Orlyval, also connects the two Orly air terminals, Orly Ouest (Orly West) and Orly Sud (Orly South), with the nearby town of Antony and Line B of the RER. Combined tickets allowing travel on

Orlyval, the RER, and the Métro are available in Métro and RER stations, and at the Orlyval stations at the airport. Just remember that Orlyval and the RER connect only at the Antony station south of Paris; frequent signs help remind you of this. The direction to take to reach Paris from the Antony station is MITRY-CLAYE or ROISSY-AÉROPORT CHARLES-DE-GAULLE; from Paris to Antony, follow the direction ST. RÉMY-LES-CHEVREUSE.

To reach Paris from the Charles de Gaulle airport, take the free airport shuttle from the air terminal to the nearby RER B station. At the RER station, simply follow the directions ROBINSON or ST. RÉMY-LES-CHEVREUSE. To reach the airport from Paris, take RER Line B and follow the direction ROISSY-AÉROPORT CHARLES-DE-GAULLE.

Two shuttle services, OrlyBus and RoissyBus,[51] also provide transportation between Paris and Orly and Charles de Gaulle airports, respectively. RoissyBus stops at the Opéra Garnier on the Right Bank of Paris. OrlyBus stops at Denfert-Rochereau on the Left Bank. RoissyBus costs €16.20; OrlyBus costs €11.20.

Allow at least 90 minutes for the trip to either airport from Paris—more if you are traveling very late or very early. Be sure to allow time for connections, too. Remember that mass transit is practical only if you have little or no luggage and are not tired after your flight; otherwise, *take a taxi.*

There is a shuttle between Paris and the airport in Beauvais,[52] for the handful of airlines based at this airport. The shuttle terminus in Paris is at Porte Maillot on the city's west side, and a ticket costs €18.00. The trip takes over an hour.

Moving about in the suburbs

If you wish to visit distant suburbs, you can use the network of suburban commuter trains, all of which are operated by the French National Railways (SNCF). Commuter trains venture further out from Paris than the RER.

Commuter trains have one of the main railway stations inside Paris as their point of departure or final destination. All of these railway stations have a Métro station below them; some of them have combined Métro and RER stations. You must leave the controlled area of the Métro or RER to make a connection, however.

The easiest way to find a train departing for your destination is to look at the departure boards in the station: just board a train for which the departure board indicates a stop at your destination. If you don't see your destination on the board, you are either at the wrong railway station or your destination station simply isn't marked (this is especially likely if the destination station is small). Check the departure displays in front of individual platforms as well, as they are more detailed in their list of stations served. If you still cannot find a train, you'll need to buy an *indicateur* (train schedule) at a newsstand in the station. Train schedules are thick little books in French, and they can be fiendishly complicated to read, so be prepared to spend some time decoding them. If you are at the wrong station, you'll have to take the Métro or RER to the correct station.

The tickets used for commuter trains are similar to those used for the Métro and RER, but they are not necessarily identical. The fare system is similar to the concentric zone system used on the RER. You can buy tickets at a ticket window, or you can buy them from machines in the station.

Tickets should be inserted into the automatic turnstiles that silently guard the commuter-train platforms. In increasingly rare cases there are no turnstiles. In still other cases, you'll need to time-punch (*composter*) your ticket in one of the little orange machines that beckon to travelers at strategic points in the station. Watch other commuters if you're not sure which of these actions is appropriate.

Whenever you venture into a railway station in search of a commuter train, keep in mind that the word BANLIEUE appears on signs referring to the suburbs, whereas GRANDES LIGNES appears on national and international rail lines. This is true for automatic ticket-dispensing machines as well. Avoid anything with GRANDES LIGNES on it unless you fancy spur-of-the-moment trips to Amsterdam or Istanbul. Helpful hint: if the ticket issued to you by a machine is roughly the size of a small envelope, you are probably buying a GRANDES LIGNES ticket; commuter tickets are the same size as Métro tickets. There is some overlap between the two for destinations in the most distant villages in the Paris region, so if you are unsure, ask for assistance at a ticket window.

Like any conventional train, a commuter train will leave and arrive at stations at predetermined times, so check schedules and departure boards. The most frequent departures take place about every fifteen minutes during rush hour, on the most heavily traveled routes. Scheduled times are usually quite well respected in practice.

An example: Getting to Disneyland Paris

Since Disneyland Paris Resort, east of the French capital, receives as many visitors as the city itself these days, instructions for reaching this popular venue may serve as an example of how to use public transport for traveling to and through the suburbs.

Disneyland Paris surrounds the Marne-la-Vallée–Chessy station on Line A of the RER. Since this station is also the eastern terminus of branch A4 of that line, you need only enter the RER and take a train in the direction of MARNE-LA-VALLÉE–CHESSY. Not all trains have this station as their terminus, so check destination boards on the platforms to make sure that the train you are boarding is headed towards the correct terminus.

Suppose that you wish to travel to Disneyland from a hotel near the Montparnasse tower on the Left Bank (south side) of Paris. The closest Métro station to this high-rise building is the Montparnasse-Bienvenüe station beneath the Montparnasse railway station. Let's also assume that you don't already have a transit pass for Zone 5. One way to proceed is as follows:

1. Enter the railway station, and follow the signs showing a Métro symbol until you find yourself in front of the entrance to the Métro. You'll need to descend by escalators or stairs from ground level inside the station.
2. At the Métro entrance, purchase a round-trip ticket (*"un aller-retour"*) for Marne-la-Vallée–Chessy. The ticket is actually two separate tickets, one to be used for the trip to Disneyland, and one to be used for the trip back (you can

use either one either way). You can purchase the ticket at the ticket window, if you speak French. You can also purchase it from a machine using coins or a credit card; the machines work in English as well as French, but they may not always accept non-French credit cards. These tickets will usually be explicitly marked with the words SECTION URBAINE and the name of the Marne-la-Vallee–Chessy destination station, meaning that they are valid for travel between any Métro station in Paris proper (that's what *section urbaine* means) and this station east of Paris.

3. Put one ticket in your pocket or wallet for later, and insert the other into a turnstile to enter the Métro. The turnstile will return the ticket; keep it with you until the end of the trip.

4. Read all signs carefully. Look for signs with the number 6 in a circle (indicating the number of the Métro line you wish to take). Some of these signs will point the way to Charles-de-Gaulle_Étoile, while others will point the way to Nation. Follow the signs that lead to Charles-de-Gaulle_Étoile. Continue this until you find yourself on a subway platform, with a sign hanging over the middle of the platform marked DIRECTION CHARLES-DE-GAULLE_ÉTOILE.

5. Wait for a train. Depending on the day of the week and the time of day, you may wait from sixty seconds to twenty minutes. The train will arrive from the left as you face the tracks.

6. When the train stops at the platform, lift the lever on the door or press the button to open it (if needed), wait until anyone leaving the train has done so, and step aboard before the buzzer sounds. The door will close automatically before the train moves.

7. Stay on the train until you reach the Charles-de-Gaulle_Étoile station. This will be the eleventh and last station on the line after departing from the Montparnasse-Bienvenüe station.

8. At Charles-de-Gaulle_Étoile, get off the train. Open the door by lifting the lever, if it has one. (Note: At this partic-

ular station, which is a terminus of Line 6, you must get off on the left side of the train.)
9. Read the signs carefully again. Look for the letter A in a circle, in red, indicating RER Line A. Follow signs pointing to Line A.
10. After walking down a few corridors, you'll find yourself confronted by turnstiles. Use the same ticket you used at Montparnasse-Bienvenüe to get through these turnstiles. The turnstile will return the ticket, so don't forget to take it back.
11. Follow the signs again, and look for the letter A in a circle, accompanied by the words Marne-la-Vallee_Chessy. When you reach the bottom of the first set of escalators, one corridor will lead to Saint-Germain-en-Laye, and another set of escalators will lead downwards towards Marne-la-Vallee_Chessy; take care to walk towards the latter.
12. Continue to follow the signs as before. Eventually, you will end up on a large platform.
13. Lighted destination boards are suspended over the platforms. Look at your destination board. If the light next to MARNE-LA-VALLEE_CHESSY is lit, the next train to arrive will take you to Marne-la-Vallee_Chessy, your destination. If this station is not lit, the next train is going elsewhere, so do not board it. If MARNE-LA-VALLÉE_CHESSY doesn't even appear on the destination board, you're on the wrong platform.
14. When a train arrives while the destination board shows MARNE-LA-VALLÉE_CHESSY as a destination, get aboard. Push the button on the door to open it, if such a button is present.
15. Take a seat, if possible; the ride is about 45 minutes long. Don't use the folding seats in the car if the car is very crowded (during rush hour, for example). Handicapped persons, pregnant women, and persons with young children (under four years of age) have priority if seating is limited, in seats so marked.
16. Stay on the train until it reaches the Marne-la-Vallee_ Chessy station, which is also the end of the line. At Marne-

la-Vallee_Chessy, get off the train. Press the button on the door to open it after the train stops, if necessary.
17. Follow the blue signs marked SORTIE until you are once again confronted by turnstiles. Use the same ticket you used to originally enter the Métro to pass through these turnstiles. The turnstile will keep your ticket, because you are leaving the RER. Since the RER station is inside Disneyland Paris Resort, you're there as soon as you walk out of the station.

Disneyland is in Zone 5, so if you have a pass rather than a single-use ticket, make sure it is good for Zone 5 before using it to travel to Disneyland. If you are only visiting the park once, buy two individual tickets, one to reach the park, and one to return to Paris; if you are visiting several days in a row, buy a multiple-use ticket. Remember that you should leave Disneyland before midnight if you don't want to miss the RER back to Paris.

Miscellaneous information

This chapter provides a bit of miscellaneous information that is handy to have when using public transportation in Paris, concerning comfort, security, regulations, etiquette, future developments and projects, and general interest.

Access for the disabled

There's both good and bad news for disabled persons who want to use Parisian mass transit, depending on the nature of their disabilities.

For persons with reduced mobility, especially those who use wheelchairs or cannot otherwise climb and descend stairs, the news is bad with respect to the Métro, but more encouraging for other modes of transportation.

Most of the Métro was designed long before access for the disabled became an issue.[53] Stairways abound in every station. Apart from the relatively new Line 14, which is 100% wheelchair-accessible, no station makes adequate provision for wheelchairs.[54] Even escalators are the exceptions rather than the rule, which means that using the Métro efficiently requires the ability to negotiate stairs. The situation is (very) gradually improving; but for now, if you use a wheelchair, you can effectively forget about the Métro—apart from Line 14, which might be worth a visit jut to see what the Métro is like at its best.

In contrast, unlike the Métro, the RER, buses, and tramways are largely accessible to wheelchairs.[55]

For travelers with impaired hearing, there are fewer issues. Many ticket windows are equipped with induction loops for use with compatible hearing aids; another option for ticket purchase is ticket machines, all of which have visual displays. On newer trains, a visual signal over or near the doors alerts deaf travelers to door closure, and visual displays indicate the name of the station for each stop.

For people with vision impairments, textured rubber strips on train platforms are common (but not universal) and can be felt with the feet or a cane. It's still a good idea to travel with a companion who can help with reading the innumerable signs in the Métro. Some lines (such as lines 1 or 14) incorporate platform doors that make it impossible to fall off the platform, but older lines have open platforms. Newer lines also have audible announcements of each station as the train arrives at the platform, although they can be hard to understand (even if you understand French). Audio announcements on the platforms of many lines advise of the approach of a train and its direction.

Service animals are allowed throughout the RER and Métro, and they ride for free. Human helpers of disabled travelers ride for free or at half price. In both cases, the disabled traveler must be carrying a French-government-issued disability card.

When it comes to buses, virtually all are equipped or designed for travelers with reduced mobility, and there are provisions for travelers with trouble hearing or seeing. Buses contain no steps and have ramps or tilt capabilities for wheelchairs. Most buses also have visual and audible announcements of each stop.

Security in the Métro

Security throughout the Parisian transit system is excellent overall. It is unlikely that you will be inconvenienced in any of these networks.[56] Police surveillance is frequent, and you will sometimes see uniformed police officers and transit-authority security agents patrolling stations and trains. Plainclothes officers and agents also are more discreetly on duty in many locations. Nevertheless, much of the petty crime affecting tourists in the city occurs in the Métro, and tourists are the most popular targets of such crime. Most incidents involve pickpocketing or stealing smartphones.

As a general rule, you should use the same common sense that you would use at home, plus extra caution to account for the fact that you are in unfamiliar surroundings. Some stations in the Métro and the RER are somewhat sketchy very late at night, just before service ends. Some stations are deserted late at night; you may be the only traveler present, and thus an obvious target. Paris has a relatively low crime rate compared to many large cities, but that doesn't mean that there is no crime at all, and tourists are always more vulnerable than the locals in any city.

It is not at all unusual for visitors to have their pockets picked or their smartphones spirited away if they are inattentive. Frequent recorded announcements in multiple languages inside the Métro warn travelers about this, and station agents may occasionally make live announcements if they spot pickpockets actively at work. Pickpockets prefer to target tourists, because they are more likely to be carrying money, and they are less likely to be paying attention, and additionally because their credit cards often don't require a PIN (all French credit cards require a secret PIN in order to be used). Rush hours, when passengers are closely packed in buses and trains, are the high-risk times for pickpocketing—buses in particular present an elevated risk. Of course, none of this is unique to Paris or its transportation system, but if you've never been in similar situations before, you should remain on guard to protect your wallet, purse, or phone. A good rule to keep in mind is that the easier it is for you to get to your wallet, the easier it is for pickpockets to steal it as well.

Thieves have been known to brazenly pluck a smartphone directly from a person's hand and run off with it. More than half of all "grab-and-run" thefts in the Métro are thefts of these prized gadgets. Cell phones and smartphones work throughout most of the Métro, but you might want to avoid using yours in situations where someone could whisk it out of your hand and disappear into the crowd.

Every Métro, RER, and commuter-train car has one or more red emergency handles near the doors. In an emergency, pulling on this handle signals the engineer and stops the train. These handles should be used only if someone is in immediate danger. The authorities have zero tolerance for pranks.

In Métro and RER stations, a small intercom, usually a yellow box with a red button, allows you to talk to the stationmaster in case of emergency. Press the button and wait for an answer, then announce which platform you are on (by giving the direction served by the platform), and explain the problem. Although it is unlikely that the stationmaster will speak English, he should still understand that something is wrong and investigate.

Trains in the Métro cannot leave the station while any of the doors on the train are open, but it is best not to test this feature of the system. The doors on the Métro are locked while the train is moving, whereas the doors on commuter trains are not; so do not attempt to open the doors on the latter until the train has stopped.

An emergency pull-tab behind a breakable window in Métro and RER stations interrupts electrical power to the rails or catenary of trains passing through the station. This device is for use only if someone actually falls onto the rails or is walking on the tracks and risks electrocution.

Regulations, schedules, amenities

There are quite a few rules and regulations governing the Métro and RER, and we list a few of the more important ones below.

If you have a camera or camcorder, be advised that transit regulations prohibit photography without a permit in the Métro and RER—but this regulation is not rigorously enforced, especially against ordinary-looking tourists.[57] Taking pictures in railway stations is fine as long as you don't use a tripod or other equipment likely to disturb other travelers, and provided that you do not stray from areas open to the public (no walking along the tracks allowed, for example). At one time you could walk onto the platforms and take pictures freely, but today you must have a ticket in hand to walk onto the platform, thanks to the increasing security paranoia of recent years.

Smoking is prohibited in all buildings open to the public in France, including all railway and subway stations. Spitting is prohibited in trains and stations.

Very large pieces of luggage are not allowed on the Métro and RER, or on buses. It isn't very practical to transport luggage in the Métro, anyway. This is the main reason why the RER isn't necessarily a good choice for getting to and from the airports, if you have any bags. Take a taxi if you have luggage.

Small dogs and cats are allowed on the Métro and RER if they are carried now, provided that they are muzzled and on a leash. The exception is service animals such as guide dogs for the blind, which are permitted everywhere and travel for free, when in the company of their owners (and appropriate documentation).

Begging and loitering are generally prohibited. Things like playing music for money, selling candy or other merchandise, and related activities, are also generally prohibited. However, some merchants and a small number of musicians have permits, and they can be recognized by the badges they wear, which are issued to them by the RATP. In fact, the RATP auditions musicians each year, and issues permits to the 300 best among them. They are allowed to play in stations, for money, but not on the platforms or in the trains.

Again, most of these regulations are virtually never enforced, so you'll see plenty of musicians playing music on trains, dogs without enclosures, sometimes people smoking, and so on.

Trains run generally from about 5 AM to at least midnight, depending on the line and station. The hours between 1 AM and 5 AM are used for maintenance on the Métro and RER, and for freight traffic on the commuter-train network. A special all-night bus service, Noctilien, is available on 47 bus routes in Paris and in some of the suburbs; it uses the same tickets as the regular Métro, with a few peculiarities.

There are no toilets on Métro and RER trains, and there are few toilets within the controlled area of the Métro and RER networks. Commuter trains may have toilets and railway stations usually have them. Most toilets are pay toilets. Some railway stations now have extremely clean public toilets with attendants, operated by outside companies, but they typically cost one or two euro per use instead of the 50 cent or so charged in other restrooms.

Technical problems interfering with Parisian mass transportation are rare, albeit not as rare as they used to be. A more frequent problem is labor strikes that cripple all or part of the system—they are one reason why Paris lost its bid for the Olympics in 2012. Especially memorable strikes occurred in 1995 and 2019. Most strikes, however, last only a day, and affect only certain Métro lines. The affected lines may stop completely or simply run trains much more slowly. The bus network is rarely affected. If only the SNCF or the RATP strikes, only the parts of the system they respectively operate will be affected.

The impact of strikes on tourists is limited because tourists can afford to simply walk within the city, and they do not usually have to be in certain places (such as an office) at certain times. A strike won't generally prevent you from getting around, but it may slow you down or make use of the Métro impractical. You'll know there's a strike when you arrive on a platform and see ten times the normal number of people waiting for a train. Public announcements are usually made as well (on video displays, and audibly).

If you arrive on a platform and there is a huge crowd of people waiting for a train, and it's not rush hour or a strike, it may be that something has temporarily delayed the trains on the line. In this case, when a train finally does arrive, it may be wise to not board it, but instead wait for the next train. The reason for this is that, when a line is temporarily delayed and then the delay is cleared, several trains in a row may arrive at very short intervals. And most people will try to board the first train that arrives, and so the trains right behind it may be nearly empty. Thus, by skipping the first train that shows up, you may be able to avoid being crammed into an overloaded train.

During rush hours, one way to cope with crowded trains is to let the first train that arrives pass, and observe the train as it leaves, noting which car has the fewest people aboard. You can then position yourself to be in front of the uncrowded car when the next train stops in the station (the pattern of crowded and uncrowded cars will usually be the same), thus providing yourself with a bit more breathing room when you board.

Métro etiquette

Parisians follow a few rules of unspoken etiquette, and it's a good idea to be aware of these and adhere to them.

On escalators and moving walkways, if you're just standing, stand to the right so that people can walk past you on the left. The people rushing past you are only gaining a few seconds by doing so, but it's still polite to stay out of their way.

During rush hour, stand to one side when a train arrives at the platform, and let people on the train get off before you try to get on. And once on the train, if it is crowded, don't use the folding seats near the doors; just remain standing instead. You can sit on the fixed seats, but keep in mind that they are further from the doors, and it can be difficult to work your way to the doors in time for your stop. And be aware that certain categories of passengers[58] have priority for certain seats that are so marked. These principles apply to buses as well.

French-English glossary

The following brief glossary lists some of the words and phrases you are most likely to encounter in the Métro, RER, or commuter-train networks. Two pronunciations are given for each term: the first being an Americanized pronunciation that isn't exact, but is easy for Americans to say; the second is the actual French pronunciation, in the International Phonetic Alphabet.

Abribus /ah-bree-booss | abʁibys/ *nm trademark* : A covered bench that provides shelter for bus riders at bus stops.

accès /ahk-say | aksɛ/ *nm* : Access. *Accès aux quais,* This way to the platforms. *Accès principal,* Main entrance. *Accès réservé aux voyageurs munis de billets,* This entrance for travelers with tickets only.

agent /ah-zhawn | aʒɑ̃/ *nm* : Agent (of transport authority). *Agent de contrôle:* transport agent who spot-checks tickets on trains or in stations.

alarme /ah-lahrm | alaʁm/ *nf* : Alarm.

aller-retour /ah-lay ruh-tour | ale ʁətuʁ/ *nm and adj* : Round (return) trip. *Un billet aller-retour,* a round-trip (return) ticket.

appareil de contrôle /ah-pah-ray duh kawn-trohl | apaʁɛj də kɔ̃tʁol/ *nm* : Turnstile, or any device used to control access to the controlled area of the MÉTRO or RER.

appoint /ah-pwan | apwɛ̃/ *nm* : *Faites l'appoint,* Use correct change.

appuyer /ah-pwee-yay | apɥije/ *vt* : Press. *Appuyer pour ouvrir,* Press to open.

APTR-ADATRIF /ah-pay-tay-ehr ah-dah-treef | apeteɛʁ adatʁif/ *nm* : former name of OPTILE.

arrêt /ah-ray | aʁɛ/ *nm* : (Bus, train) stop. *Arrêts desservis,* Stops served (by bus, train). *Arrêt demandé,* Stop requested (of bus driver). *Marquer l'arrêt,* To make a stop (on a bus or train route).

arrière /ahr-ee-air | aʁjɛʁ/ *nm* : Rear. *Arrière des trains courts,* Trailing end of short trains (on RER and commuter platforms).

arrivée /ahr-ee-vay | aʁive/ *nf* : Arrival; destination.

attentif /ahr-tawn-teef | atɑ̃tif/ *adj* : Aware. *Attentifs, ensemble,* Everyone aware (safety slogan).

avant /ah-vawn | avɑ̃/ *nm* : Front. *Avant des trains courts,* Front of short trains (on RER and commuter platforms).

banlieue /bahn-leeyuh | bɑ̃ljø/ *nf* : Suburb. *Train de banlieue,* Suburban commuter train.

billet /bee-yeh | bijɛ/ *nm* : TICKET. *Billets,* tickets. *Limite de validité des billets,* Tickets no longer valid beyond this point. *Accès limité aux voyageurs munis de billets,* This entrance for travelers with tickets only. *Billet non valable,* Ticket expired or ticket invalid. *Reprenez votre billet,* Take back your ticket.

carnet /kar-neh | kaʁnɛ/ *nm* : Pack of five or ten cardboard tickets.

Carte Améthyste /kart ah-may-teest | kaʁt ametist/ *nf trademark* : A transit pass issued to certain Parisian senior citizens, handicapped persons, and war veterans that allows free or discount access to the entire Parisian mass-transit system throughout the metropolitan area.

Carte Émeraude /kart aim-road | kaʁt emʁod/ *nf trademark* : A transit pass issued to certain Parisian senior citizens, handicapped persons, and war veterans that allows free or discount access to the entire Parisian mass-transit system with Paris alone.

Carte Orange /kart oh-rawnzh | kaʁt oʁɑ̃ʒ/ *nf trademark* : An obsolete but legendary transit pass, predecessor of the NAVIGO card, sold between 1975 and 2009.

Carte Rubis /kart roo-bee | kaʁt ʁybi/ *nf trademark* : A transit pass issued to certain Parisian senior citizens, handicapped persons, and war veterans that allows free or discount access to the mass transit within the Paris region on lines operated by OPTILE only.

Public Transportation in Paris

¹**cent** /sent | sɛnt/ *nm* : A unit of currency equal to 1/100 of a euro. *Treize euros et trente cents,* €13.30.

²**cent** /sawn | sã/ *adj* : (One) hundred.

centime /sawn-teem | sãtim/ *nm* : 1. ¹Cent. 2. A unit of the old French national currency (no longer legal tender) equal to 1/100 of a French franc (about €0.0015).

chantier /shawnt-yay | ʃãtje/ *nm* : Construction zone. *Chantier interdit,* Construction zone—keep out.

chef /shef | ʃɛf/ *nm* : *Chef de station,* Stationmaster. *Pour appeler le chef de station,* Press here to call stationmaster.

colis /koh-lee | kɔli/ *nm* : Package. *Signalez tout colis suspect,* Report any suspect package.

composter /kawn-pohs-tay | kɔ̃pɔste/ *vt* : To validate or time-punch a ticket.

contrôle /kawn-trohl | kɔ̃tʁol/ *nm* : Inspection. *Agent de contrôle:* RATP agent responsible for checking that everyone in the MÉTRO is carrying a valid ticket or *titre de transport. Appareil de contrôle:* turnstile.

correspondance /kor-es-pawn-dawnss | kɔʁɛspɔ̃dãs/ *nf* : Connection (*e.g.*, between trains). *Prendre la correspondance sur le quai,* Descend to the platform to make connections.

coupon /koo-pawn | kupɔ̃/ *nm* : a (cardboard) TICKET, especially one that is valid for more than one trip.

Découverte /day-koo-vehrt | dekuvɛʁt/ : NAVIGO DÉCOUVERTE.

défense /day-fawns | defãs/ *nf* : Prohibition. *Défense de fumer,* Smoking prohibited. *Défense d'entrer,* No admittance. *La Défense:* A high-rise business district just northwest of Paris.

départ /day-pahr | depaʁ/ *nm* : Departure.

descente /day-sawnt | desãt/ *nf* : *Descente interdite,* Do not get off the train on this side.

desservi /day-sehr-vee | desɛʁvi/ *pp* : Served. *Cet arrêt n'est pas desservi le dimanche,* this stop is not served on Sundays.

dézonage /day-zohn-ahzh | dezonaʒ/ *nm* : Temporary or permanent validity of a ticket or pass over multiple ZONES that are not normally included with that ticket or pass.

direction /dee-rehks-yawn | diʁɛksjɔ̃/ *nf* : Direction (of travel); the station that is the terminus of a given train.

Easy /ee-zee | izi/ : NAVIGO EASY.

French-English Glossary

Éole /ay-ohl | eɔl/ *nf trademark* : Line E of the RER.

euro /euh-roh | œʁo/ *nm* : The unit of currency throughout France and most of the European Union, with a value close to that of one U.S. dollar.

Eurostar /uh-roh-star | œʁostaʁ/ *nm trademark* : A special TGV train that connects France and the United Kingdom via the Channel Tunnel.

exact /egg-zahkt | egzakt/ *adj* : Correct. *Mettez la somme exacte,* Use correct change.

fermé /fehr-may | fɛʁme/ *adj* : Closed.

forfait annuel /for-feh ah-noo-ehl | foʁfɛ anyɛl/ *nm* : A yearly transit pass, recorded on a NAVIGO card, and valid for travel during one calendar year within specified ZONES.

forfait jour /for-feh zhoor | foʁfɛ ʒuʁ/ *nm* : A one-day transit pass, recorded on a NAVIGO card, and valid for travel during one day within specified ZONES.

forfait mois /for-feh mwah | foʁfɛ mwa/ *nm* : A monthly transit pass, recorded on a NAVIGO card, and valid for travel during one calendar month within specified ZONES.

forfait semaine /for-feh suh-mehn | foʁfɛ səmɛn/ *nm* : A weekly transit pass, recorded on a NAVIGO card, and valid for travel during one calendar week, Monday through Sunday, within specified ZONES.

gare /gahr | gaʁ/ *nf* : (Railway) station. *Gares desservies,* Stations served.

grève /grehv | gʁɛv/ *nf* : Labor strike. *En grève,* on strike.

IDFM /ee-day-eff-em | ideɛfɛm/ *abbrev* : *Île-de-France Mobilités,* or Regonal Paris Mobility, the umbrella organization managing all the public-transit operators in the Paris metropolitan area; formerly STIF.

Imagine "R" /ee-mah-zheen air | imaʒin ɛʁ/ *nm trademark* : A type of low-cost annual transit pass sold exclusively to resident students under 26 years of age.

incident /an-see-dawn | ɛ̃sidɑ̃/ *nm* : Incident; problem. *Suite à un incident grave de voyageur, le traffic est totalement interrompu,* Because of a serious passenger accident, train service has been completely suspended.

indicateur /an-dee-cah-tuhr | ɛ̃dikatœʁ/ *nm* : Train schedule.

interdit /an-tehr-dee | ɛ̃tɛʁdi/ *adj* : Prohibited. *Passage interdit,* Wrong way. *Interdit au public,* No admittance. *Stationnement interdit,* No loitering. *Fumer interdit,* Smoking prohibited.

jour /zhoor | ʒuʁ/ *nm* : Day.

Liberté+ /lib-ehr-tay ploos | libɛʁte plys/ : NAVIGO LIBERTÉ+.

ligne /leen | liɲ/ *nf* : Line. *Grandes lignes,* National/international rail network. *Lignes de banlieue,* suburban (commuter) rail lines.

Météor /may-tay-or | meteoʁ/ *nm trademark (rare)* : Line 14 of the MÉTRO.

Métro /may-troh | metʁo/ *nm* : The conventional subway network serving the city of Paris proper. Also called the RÉSEAU URBAIN (city network).

microbus /mee-kroh-booss | mikʁobys/ *nm* : A very small bus with a capacity of 22 passengers that serves certain lightly-traveled bus routes.

Mobilis /moh-bee-lees | mobilis/ *nm trademark* : A type of one-day multiple-use ticket.

mois /mwah | mwa/ *adj* : Month. (See FORFAIT MOIS.)

Monmartrobus /mon-mar-troh-boos | mɔ̃maʁtʁobys/ *nm trademark* : Former name of bus line 40, which serves the neighborhood of Montmartre.

monnaie /muh-nay | mɔnɛ/ *nf* : Change. *Je rends la monnaie,* I can make change.

mouvement social /moov-mawn sohss-yal | muvmɑ̃ sosjal/ *nm (official term)* : Labor strike.

Navigo /nah-vee-goh | navigo/ *nm trademark* : A type of reloadable "smart card" pass that does not require physical insertion into a turnstile.

Navigo Découverte /nah-vee-goh day-koo-vairt | navigo dekuvɛʁt/ *nm trademark* : A type of NAVIGO pass, available to anyone but usable by only one person, that can store several types of prepaid trip passes.

Navigo Easy /nah-vee-goh ee-zee | navigo izi/ *nm trademark* : A type of NAVIGO pass, available to anyone, that can store a variable number of individual prepaid tickets or passes.

French-English glossary

Navigo Liberté+ /nah-vee-goh lib-ehr-tay | navigo libɛʁte/ *nm trademark* : A type of NAVIGO card that bills for trips after the fact, intended for local residents.

Noctambus /nohk-tahm-booss | nɔktambys/ *nm trademark* : See NOCTILIEN.

Noctilien /nohk-teel-yan | nɔktiljɛ̃/ *nm trademark* : A nighttime network of 47 bus routes that serves Paris and some suburbs during the night and replaces the old NOCTAMBUS network.

OpenTour /oh-pen-toor | opɛn tuʁ/ *nm trademark* : Former name of TOOTBUS.

OPTILE /up-teel | ɔptil/ *nm trademark* : A group of transit systems affiliated with the RATP and serving mostly the Paris suburbs, formerly APTR-ADATRIF.

origine-destination /oh-ree-zheen dehs-tee-nah-syawn | ɔʁiʒin dɛstinasjɔ̃/ *adj inv* : Used to identify a TICKET that is valid only between two specific stations.

OrlyBus /or-lee-booss | ɔʁlibys/ *nm trademark* : A shuttle bus service between Paris and Orly airport.

OrlyRail /or-lee-rye | ɔʁliʁaj/ *nm* : A former rail service between Paris and Orly airport, now merged into Line C of the RER.

Orlyval /or-lee-vahl | ɔʁlival/ *nm trademark* : A fully automated light rail system that serves Orly Airport and connects with the Antony station of the RER.

ouvert /oo-vehr | uvɛʁ/ *adj* : Open.

Paris Visite /pah-ree vee-zeet | paʁi vizit/ *nm trademark* : A type of multiple-use ticket intended for tourists.

partie /pahr-tee | paʁti/ *nf* : *Partie de train restant en gare,* This part of the train remains in the station.

passage /pah-sahj | pasaʒ/ *nm* : Passageway. *Passage interdit,* Wrong way. *Passage public,* Pedestrian underpass.

plan /plaw | plɑ̃/ *nm* : Map. *Plan indicateur lumineux d'itinéraires (PILI),* illuminated interactive map, present in some stations.

portillon /por-tee-yawn | pɔʁtijɔ̃/ *nm* : *Portillon automatique,* an automatic door used to regulate access to a MÉTRO platform—no longer used but still present in some stations.

première classe /prum-yehr klahss | pʁəmjɛʁ klas/ *nf* : First class. *Vous êtes en première classe,* you're in first class.

quai /kay | ke/ *nm* : Platform. *Accès aux quais,* This way to the platforms.

rame /rahm | ʁam/ *nf (RATP)* : Train; specifically, a self-powered, double-ended trainset of the type used in the MÉTRO. *Rame à quai,* train at the platform.

RATP /err-ah-tay-pay | εʁatepe/ *nf abbrev* : Régie Autonome des Transports Parisiens, Autonomous Paris Transport Authority.

repère /ruh-pair | ʁəpεʁ/ *nm* : Marker; indication painted on a platform to show where a given car stops.

RER /air-uh-air | εʁəεʁ/ *nm abbrev* : The *Réseau Express Régional,* or Regional Express Network, a system of high-speed subways that interconnect with the MÉTRO.

réseau urbain /ray-zoh oor-nan | ʁezo yʁbε̃/ *nm* : The part of the rail transit network that serves Paris proper.

Roissy /rwah-see | ʁwasi/ *nm* : Short for *Roissy-en-France,* a village next to Charles de Gaulle airport; often used informally to refer to the airport itself.

RoissyBus /rwah-see-booss | ʁwasibys/ *nm* : A shuttle bus service between Paris and Charles de Gaulle airport.

RoissyRail /rwah-see-rye | ʁwasiʁaj/ *nm* : A former rail service between Paris and Charles de Gaulle airport, now merged into Line B of the RER.

semaine /suh-mehn | səmεn/ *adj* : Week. (See FORFAIT SEMAINE.)

SNCF /ess-en-say-eff | εsεnseεf/ *nf abbrev* : Société Nationale des Chemins de Fer Français, French National Railway Company.

section /sehk-syawn | sεksjɔ̃/ *nf* : A fare segment of a bus route. *Section urbaine:* The portion of the Parisian transit system that is within the actual city limits of Paris.

secours /suh-koor | səkuʁ/ *nm* : Help. *Au secours!* Help!

service /sehr-vees | sεʁvis/ *nm* : Service. *Hors service,* Out of order. *En service,* Ready for use. *Service interrompu,* Service discontinued. *Service perturbé,* Delays expected. *Réservé au service,* Authorized personnel only. *Service normal,* Standard service. *Service spécial,* Non-scheduled service. *Service partiel,* Partial service. *Service restreint,* Limited service.

sortie /sor-tee | soʁti/ *nf* : Exit. *Sortie de secours,* Emergency exit.

station /stah-syawn | stasjɔ̃/ *nf* : Station.

French-English glossary

STIF /es-tay-ee-ef | ɛsteiɛf/ *nm abbrev* : *Syndicat des Transports d'Île-de-France,* Paris Metropolitan Transport Syndicate, renamed IDFM in 2017.

sauvette /soh-veht | sovɛt/ *nf* : *Vente (des billets) à la sauvette:* Illegal resale (of tickets), as by unauthorized persons in the subway system.

tarification /tah-ree-fee-kah-syawn | taʁifikasjɔ̃/ *nf* : *Tarification spéciale,* Special tickets required.

terminus /tehr-mee-noos | tɛʁminys/ *nm* : Terminus; end of the line.

TGV /tay-zhay-vay | teʒeve/ *nm abbrev* : *Train à Grande Vitesse,* a very high-speed (300-kph/200-mph) full-size train operated on many national and international rail lines by the SNCF.

Thalys /tah-lees | talis/ *nm trademark* : A special TGV train that serves primarily Belgium.

ticket /tee-keh | tikɛ/ *nm* : a standard MÉTRO single-use ticket; BILLET.

ticket t+ /tee-keh tay ploos | tikɛ te plys/ *nm* : a single-use ticket that allows unlimited changes among most rail, tram, and bus lines for one trip over a limited period (two hours for rail, 90 minutes for buses).

Ticket Jeunes /tee-keh zhuhn | tikɛ ʒœn/ *nm trademark* : A multiple-use ticket for persons under age 26 and valid only on weekends and holidays for selected ZONES.

titre de transport /teetruh duh trawns-pohr | titʁə də tʁɑ̃spoʁ/ *nm (RATP)* : Ticket or pass allowing access to pubic transportation.

Tootbus /toot-boos | tutbys/ *nm trademark* : A fleet of double-decker open-top sightseeing buses owned and operated by a subsidiary of the RATP.

totem /toh-tem | totɛm/ *nm* : A freestanding sign on a pole marking the entrance to a MÉTRO or RER station, or a bus or tram stop.

train /tran | tʁɛ̃/ *nm* : Train. *Train court,* Short train. *Train long,* Full-length train. *Avant du train,* The first car of the train stops here. *Arrière du train,* The last car of the train ends here. *Avant des trains courts,* Short trains start here. *Arrière des trains* *courts,* Short trains end here. *Train à quai,* The train is at the platform. *Train à l'approche,* The train is entering the station.

Transilien /trawn-seel-yan | tʁɑ̃siljɛ̃/ *nm trademark* : The rail network of the Paris region as operated by the SNCF.

travaux /trah-voh | tʁavo/ *nm pl* : Works; construction. *Secteur en travaux,* Construction area.

tripode /tree-pud | tʁipɔd/ *nm (RATP)* : Turnstile (the kind with three rotating arms).

valider /vahl-ee-day | valide/ *vt* : To insert a ticket into an automatic turnstile or wave a Navigo pass at the turnstile, officially entering the transit system.

vigilant /vee-zhee-lawn | viʒilɑ̃/ *adj* : Vigilant. *Soyons vigilants ensemble,* Let's all be watchful.

Vigipirate /vee-zhee-pee-raht | viʒipiʁat/ *adj service mark* : *Plan Vigipirate:* A government program to reduce the incidence of terrorist attacks in the country, as by closing trash cans or sanisettes, or other security measures.

voie /vwah | vwa/ *nf* : Right-of-way; track. *Interdiction de traverser les voies,* Crossing the tracks is prohibited. *Départ voie A,* Departure on track A.

voiture /vwah-toor | vwatyʁ/ *nf* : Car. *Troisième voiture,* Third car (of a train).

wagon /vah-gon | vagɔ̃/ *nm* : Car (of a train). *Troisième wagon,* Third car (of a train).

voyageur /vwah-yah-zhuhr | vwajaʒœʁ/ *nm* : Passenger. *Ce train ne prend plus de voyageurs,* This train is no longer in service.

zone /zohn | zon/ *nf* : Zone. *Zone tarifaire:* One of the five concentric transit-fare zones centered on Paris, and numbered outwards from Paris (the city itself is Zone 1). *Zone contrôlée:* The area of the MÉTRO within which a valid ticket is required.

NOTES

1 About 50.3 million in 2019, according to the *Comité Régional du Tourisme,* the INSEE, and AirDNA; and, after a precipitous drop during the Covid hysteria of 2020 and 2021, the numbers are climbing even higher now.
2 This is not a joke. The entrance is across the street from the Pont de l'Alma RER station. Admission is €9.
3 This includes eight million commutes by rail, and 1.3 million by bus and tramway. Ten percent of users are tourists.
4 The population of the Paris metropolitan area is about twelve million, making it the size of Los Angeles, and larger than London, depending on how you count.
5 *Métro* is short for *chemin de fer métropolitain,* "metropolitan railroad."
6 Typographic conventions vary on how to separate two or more names when they are strung together to identify a Métro station. In this book, we've simply adopted the en dash, but you may see many variations in the field.
7 Except, it seems, when going to or from the airports—at least some visitors believe they are being very clever by schlepping their luggage trough the subway for two hours. Ironically, this is one occasion when it makes a lot more sense to take a taxi. Even more ironically, these same visitors might well eschew public transportation at any other time during their stay.
8 RER stands for *réseau express régional,* or "regional express network." Parisians pronounce this as three separate letters, *i.e.,* "err-uh-err."
9 In case you're wondering, the two most popular suburban attractions, Versailles and Disneyland, are both reachable directly via the RER.
10 The tramway lines are designated T1, T2, T3a, T3b, T4, T5, T6, T7, T7, T8, T11, and T13.
11 RATP stands for *Régie autonome des transports parisiens,* "Independent Parisian Transport Authority."
12 SNCF stands for *Société Nationale des Chemins de Fer français,* "French National Railway Company."
13 IDFM stands for *Île-de-France Mobilités.* Until 2017 it was called *Syndicat des Transports d'Île-de-France,* or *STIF.*
14 *Metro* is a common name for a subway system worldwide, however, and

Public Transportation in Paris

not all systems called metros were inspired by the Parisian version.

15 The lines are designated 1, 2, 3, 3bis, 4, 5, 6, 7, 7bis, 8, 9, 10, 11, 12, 13, and 14. Lines 15 and 16 are under construction.

16 The city of Paris proper is roughly oval and is largely delimited by a beltway that surrounds the city. It's only a few miles across. The rest of the substantial metropolitan area is suburbs.

17 On lines 7bis and 10, there are a few stations that are served only by trains going in one direction.

18 There are a few exceptions. The last station with restricted opening hours, Liège, adopted the same hours as all other stations in 2006. The Rennes station had done the same in 2004. However, Lines 7 and 13 also separate into two branches near the city limits, and you must check signs on the platforms, in the stations, or on the trains to be sure you are on the correct branch to reach your destination. Lines 10 and 7bis include a few physically separated stations stations that are served only in one direction.

19 No point within the city limits is more than 300 yards from a Métro station, and typically they are much closer.

20 This limit is extended to two hours for cardboard single-use tickets.

21 These exceptions are usually trips between stations around the edge of the city, because of the star-shaped layout of the lines and the lack of a line around the perimeter of the city..

22 This is the author's own estimate, based on experience. Official average figures usually concern commuting to or from work, and tend to be considerably longer—and misleading for our purposes here—because they involve the suburbs.

23 Exceptions include Métro lines 7 and 13.

24 RER stations in Paris are technically separate from Métro stations, and may have slightly different names; but they are connected to the Métro by corridors so that you can easily make connections between the Métro and RER without leaving the system. For example, there are two Métro stations called Les Halles and Châtelet, and they connect directly with the aptly-named RER station Châtelet–Les Halles, forming one huge underground station—which incidentally is the largest of its kind in the world.

25 These are called *origine-destination* tickets, and are valid only between two specific stations.

26 The RER doesn't lead directly to the terminals at the airports, but merely nearby—thanks to intense lobbying by taxi drivers, who were afraid that stations right in the terminals would significantly erode their lucrative airport business. The fixed price for a taxi from Charles de Gaulle airport and the Left Bank of Paris, for example, is €58 at the time of this writing.

27 Specifically, H, J, K, L, N, P, R, and U.

28 Métro lines serve all the railway stations in Paris. The RER serves all but the

Notes

Montparnasse and Est railway stations, and there's a short walk (within the system) between RER Line E and the Saint-Lazare railway station.

29 If you're wondering when you might use these commuter trains, they can come in handy for visits to places like Fontainebleau (Ligne R) or Monet's garden in Giverny (Line J). For still more distant destinations, such as Lyon or Nice, you'd simply use the national railways.

30 With an area of less than 34 square miles, Paris is smaller than its own Charles de Gaulle airport to the north.

31 There is a complex and arcane logic behind the numbering of the bus routes, but we leave exploration of the details as an exercise for the reader.

32 Lines T4, T11, and T13 are operated by the SNCF or one of its subsidiaries as part of the Transilien network; the others are operated by the RATP.

33 Although this really *was* a funicular—that is, a pair of cars hoisted by cables and counterweighting reach other—when it was built in 1900, that was long ago replaced by independently-hoisted cars, and the system retains *funicular* in its name only, for historical reasons.

34 Called Louise Michel Square, if you are curious.

35 A one-day pass costs €17 for an adult.

36 A one-day pass costs €35.10 for an adult.

37 Branded as the *ticket t+* by the transit authorities.

38 More specifically, any trip confined to the Métro and/or the RER in Zone 1, including connections; or any trip confined to buses (except OrlyBus and RoissyBus) and/or trams, including connections.

39 This can also vary depending on the line you take. For example, you can travel to La Défense with an ordinary Métro ticket if you take Line 1, but if you take RER A, the fare changes. This is probably linked to the fact that Métro stations do not have exit turnstiles that can check the ticket type, whereas the (much younger) RER stations do.

40 Or a year, for residents.

41 At €65.80 for five days, and five zones, the Paris Visite pass is nearly three times more expensive than the equivalent weekly Navigo pass.

42 Often with a sign saying LIMITE DE VALIDITÉ DES BILLETS. If you are leaving the RER, this exit will usually be a turnstile that requires you to use your ticket or pass again to get out (because the RER has multiple fare zones that are rechecked at the exits).

43 The actual amount can vary with the precise violation and the circumstances, ranging from €5 to €375.

44 The cardboard tickets contain information recorded on a magnetic stripe. Although it's rare, the stripe can be demagnetized if brought into close proximity to the extremely strong magnets used for magnetic clasps on some personal accessories. Navigo cards contain microprocessors and communicate using the contactless Calypso standard, and are not sensitive to magnetic fields.

45 If you're expensing transportation, be advised that both ticket windows and ticket machines provide receipts. Those from machines often resemble an extra-long cardboard ticket.

46 Trams are grouped wit buses in this context.

47 The reader will wonder why there are no maps in this book. There are several reasons. A map that will fit into a paperback or e-book tends to have microscopic print. A fold-out mp is complicated and expensive to print. A map also has to be licensed and royalties paid, which raises the price of the book and complicates publication. There are maps everywhere at Métro stations. And finally, Métro apps providing maps or itineraries are so common that placing a map inside a book is redundant

48 The exceptions are Line 2 and Line 6, both of which have an eastern terminus at the Nation station. For this reason, signs in places where the two lines might be confused specify directions as NATION PAR DENFERT-ROCHEREAU for Line 6, or NATION PAR BARBÈS-ROCHECHOUART for Line 2 (Denfert-Rochereau and Barbès-Rochechouart are stations on Line 6 and Line 2, respectively). Line 2 arcs through the northern half of the city (the Right Bank); Line 6 follows a similar curving path through the southern half of the city (the Left Bank).

49 This tends to happen most commonly when you are trying to travel between two stations along the edge of the city, because most lines branch approximately outwards from the center of town, with only two following a path *around* the center.

50 Be especially aware on Line 6 at the Charles de Gaulle_Étoile station, at the top of the Champs-Élysées. Everyone gets off on the left; if you get off on the right, you won't be able to find the exit.

51 Charles de Gaulle airport partly impinges on the village of Roissy-en-France, and so the airport is often referred to as *Roissy* for short.

52 Generously referred to as Paris-Beauvais, even though Beauvais is 85 kilometers away from Paris—almost half the disstance to the English Channel.

53 The space underneath Paris is so crowded that there's literally no room for elevators in many existing stations. Line 14 gt around this by being built *underneath* everything else—which is why you must descend nine or ten stories on elevators or escalators in order to reach the trains. Bright interior lighting helps create the impression that the line isn't as deep as it actually is.

54 Although some other stations do have elevators, their lack of other necessary adaptations makes them unusable for wheelchair users, for all practical purposes.

55 All RER stations on lines A and B are accessible, and lines C, D, and E should be 100% accessible by 2024. All buses inside Paris, and three out of four buses in the suburbs, are accessible to wheelchairs. All tramways are accessible.

56 During the first ten months of 2019, there were nearly 8000 thefts in the Métro and RER—an increase of 59% over the preceding year—but that

Notes

still corresponds to only one passenger in 300,000 being victimized.

57 The fine is €60, if they decide to enforce it.
58 These categories are, in declining order of priority: people with war or military injuries; legally blind people; people who cannot work for medical reasons; people who cannot stand for long periods; pregnant women; people accompanying children younger than four years of age; disabled people not specifically designated as being unable to stand for long periods; persons with a card saying that they cannot stand for long periods; and people aged 75 or older.

Printed in Great Britain
by Amazon